Types of Precipitation

By NADIA HIGGINS
Illustrations by SARA INFANTE
Music by ERIK KOSKINEN

CANTATA
LEARNING

WWW.CANTATALEARNING.COM

CANTATA
LEARNING

Published by Cantata Learning
1710 Roe Crest Drive
North Mankato, MN 56003
www.cantatalearning.com

Library of Congress Control Number: 2017007535
978-1-68410-057-6 (hardcover/CD)
978-1-68410-078-1 (paperback)

Types of Precipitation by Nadia Higgins
Illustrated by Sara Infante
Music by Erik Koskinen

Book design, Tim Palin Creative
Editorial direction, Flat Sole Studio
Executive musical production and direction, Elizabeth Draper
Music arranged and produced by Erik Koskinen

Printed in the United States of America in North Mankato, Minnesota.
072017   0367CGF17

ACCESS THE MUSIC!

SCAN CODE WITH MOBILE APP

CANTATALEARNING.COM

TIPS TO SUPPORT LITERACY AT HOME

WHY READING AND SINGING WITH YOUR CHILD IS SO IMPORTANT

Daily reading with your child leads to increased academic achievement. Music and songs, specifically rhyming songs, are a fun and easy way to build early literacy and language development. Music skills correlate significantly with both phonological awareness and reading development. Singing helps build vocabulary and speech development. And reading and appreciating music together is a wonderful way to strengthen your relationship.

READ AND SING EVERY DAY!

TIPS FOR USING CANTATA LEARNING BOOKS AND SONGS DURING YOUR DAILY STORY TIME

1. As you sing and read, point out the different words on the page that rhyme. Suggest other words that rhyme.

2. Memorize simple rhymes such as Itsy Bitsy Spider and sing them together. This encourages comprehension skills and early literacy skills.

3. Use the questions in the back of each book to guide your singing and storytelling.

4. Read the included sheet music with your child while you listen to the song. How do the music notes correlate to the words of the song?

5. Sing along on the go and at home. Access music by scanning the QR code on each Cantata book. You can also stream or download the music for free to your computer, smartphone, or mobile device.

Devoting time to daily reading shows that you are available for your child. Together, you are building language, literacy, and listening skills.

Have fun reading and singing!

Precipitation happens when water **droplets** fall from the clouds. It can come in four types. Rain and snow are two forms of precipitation. **Sleet** happens when rain freezes as it's falling. **Hail** occurs when rain freezes into balls of ice high up in storm clouds.

Turn the page to learn all about the different types of precipitation. Remember to sing along!

Rain and snow, sleet and hail,
all water drops from the sky.

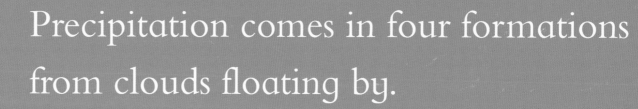

Precipitation comes in four formations
from clouds floating by.

In a cloud, droplets combine.

They get heavy. Down they fall.

8

Pitter-patter, pitter-patter.
Rain taps on the wall.

9

In a cloud, ice **crystals** make flakes
so fat they cannot float.

Flutter–glide. Flutter–glide.
Snow falls on the road.

11

Rain and snow, sleet and hail,
all water drops from the sky.

Precipitation comes in four formations
from clouds floating by.

13

From a cloud, wet raindrops fall.

But they freeze on their way down.

Plunkety-plunk. Plunkety-plunk.
Icy sleet hits the ground.

15

In thunder clouds, rain starts to freeze into balls of ice that grow and grow.

Crash-bang! Clackety-clang!
Hail knocks on the window.

17

Hear the rain splat, rat-a-tat, rat-a-tat!

Feel the cold snow from your head to your toes.

See the slick sleet as it bounces on the street.

Make a mad dash when the hail starts to crash.

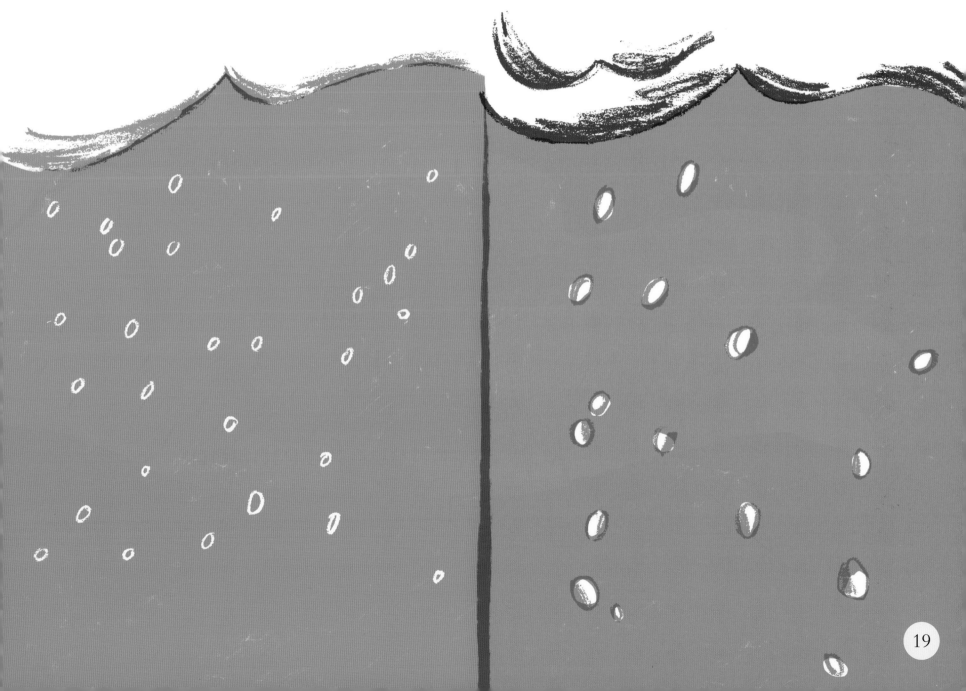

Rain and snow, sleet and hail,
all water drops from the sky.

Precipitation comes in four formations
from clouds floating by.

Rain and snow, sleet and hail,
all water drops from the sky.

Precipitation comes in four formations
from clouds floating by.

SONG LYRICS
Types of Precipitation

Rain and snow, sleet and hail,
all water drops from the sky.
Precipitation comes in four formations
from clouds floating by.

In a cloud, droplets combine.
They get heavy. Down they fall.
Pitter-patter, pitter-patter.
Rain taps on the wall.

In a cloud, ice crystals make flakes
so fat they cannot float.
Flutter-glide. Flutter-glide.
Snow falls on the road.

Rain and snow, sleet and hail,
all water drops from the sky.
Precipitation comes in four formations
from clouds floating by.

From a cloud, wet raindrops fall.
But they freeze on their way down.
Plunkety-plunk. Plunkety-plunk.
Icy sleet hits the ground.

In thunder clouds, rain starts to freeze
into balls of ice that grow and grow.
Crash-bang! Clackety-clang!
Hail knocks on the window.

Hear the rain splat, rat-a-tat-tat!
Feel the cold snow from your head to your toes.
See the slick sleet as it bounces on the street.
Make a mad dash when the hail starts to crash.

Rain and snow, sleet and hail,
all water drops from the sky.
Precipitation comes in four formations
from clouds floating by.

Rain and snow, sleet and hail,
all water drops from the sky.
Precipitation comes in four formations
from clouds floating by.

Types of Precipitation

Americana
Erik Koskinen

Chorus

Rain and snow, sleet and hail, all wa - ter drops from the sky. Pre -
cip - i - ta - tion comes in four for - ma - tions from clouds float-ing by. by.

Verse

1. In a cloud, drop - lets com - bine. They get heav-y. Down they fall.
Pit - ter - pat - ter, pit - ter - pat - ter. Rain taps on the wall.

Verse 2
In a cloud, ice crystals make flakes
so fat they cannot float.
Flutter-glide. Flutter-glide.
Snow falls on the road.

Chorus

Verse 3
From a cloud, wet raindrops fall.
But they freeze on their way down.
Plunkety-plunk. Plunkety-plunk.
Icy sleet hits the ground.

Verse 4
In thunder clouds, rain starts to freeze
into balls of ice that grow and grow.
Crash-bang! Clackety-clang!
Hail knocks on the window.

Bridge

Hear the rain splat, rat - a - tat - tat! Feel the cold snow from your head to your toes.
See the slick sleet as it bounc - es on the street. Make a mad dash when the hail starts to crash.

Chorus (x2)

GLOSSARY

crystals—glass-like substances that have many sides and are see through

dash—to run

droplets—very small drops of liquid

formations—things that are created

hail—small balls or lumps of ice that fall from the sky

sleet—frozen rain

GUIDED READING ACTIVITIES

1. Rain, snow, sleet, and hail are the four kinds of precipitation. Which is your favorite and why?

2. In which season does rain happen most? When does it usually snow? Have you ever seen sleet or hail? What season was it?

3. Draw a picture of people out in the rain or snow. What type of clothes do they need to wear?

TO LEARN MORE

Cannons, Heather Cox. *Rain*. North Mankato, MN: Heinemann-Raintree, 2015.

Cannons, Heather Cox. *Snow*. North Mankato, MN: Heinemann-Raintree, 2015.

Meister, Cari, *Kit and Mateo Journey Into the Clouds: Learning About Clouds*. North Mankato, MN: Capstone, 2014.

Schuetz, Kristin. *Precipitation*. Minnetonka, MN: Bellweather Media, 2014.